New/Revised

# Football Rules
# IN PICTURES

Edited by Don Schiffer and Lud Duroska

Foreword by Mel Hein SUPERVISOR OF OFFICIALS,
AMERICAN FOOTBALL CONFERENCE

Introduction by Clary Anderson HEAD FOOTBALL COACH,
MONTCLAIR STATE COLLEGE

*Illustrated by George Kraynak*

GROSSET & DUNLAP    *PUBLISHERS*    NEW YORK

*Dedicated to*
*Helen, Marilyn and Jeffrey*

*The authors wish to express their appreciation of the help given so generously by the National Collegiate Athletic Association; the National Federation of State High School Athletic Associations; the National Football League, Jim Heffernan, Jack Horrigan and Mel Hein; and Steve Gerdy.*

## A GREAT SPORT

Football, on the field and off, has been the dominant factor in my life. It has taught me discipline and team play . . . it has taught me that there are winners and losers, and that winners don't always keep winning, nor do losers always keep losing.

I can think of no better training for a productive life than competition in football on the high school, college and professional levels. The sport demands desire and ability to take the initiative. Strength is necessary but so is courage. Characteristics like these are most necessary if a man is to lead a productive and meaningful life for himself and his family.

Persons in the stands profit from football, too, and this goes beyond those few hours of entertainment. They are made aware of the necessity of a man's combining his top physical and mental qualities for ultimate success. Brought home, too, as they watch the flow of action which has been described as everything from a master chess game to a "war without casualties" is the realization that, all things being equal, eleven men attuned to each other and aware of the other man's position must ultimately come out ahead of eleven individualists.

Mel Hein, All-America at Washington State, starred for fifteen years, 1931–45, as center and linebacker (those were pre-two-platoon days) for the New York Giants. In 1938 he was voted the Most Valuable Player in the National Football League, the only interior lineman to be so honored. He is a member of both the College and Pro Football Halls of Fame, and was a charter member of the Pro Football Hall of Fame.

# CONTENTS

# THE IMPORTANCE OF KNOWING THE RULES

In the courtroom a Judge often has to tell an offender that "Ignorance of the Law is no excuse." How true in sports!

I doubt that there is a coach who doesn't remember a game that was lost because a player didn't know a rule and committed a violation. The player's intentions may have been thoroughly honest, but the officials have to go by the "law" — the rules of the game — and the needless penalty determined the outcome of the contest.

That is one of the reasons why a book such as this one, devoted as it is to interpreting and clarifying the fundamental rules of football, is an important aid to the player who is learning the game. Through the illustrations and the explanations, he learns what can and what cannot be done. The devise of having offensive players in white jerseys and the defensive players in black helps make the action easier to follow.

The more thoroughly a player learns the rules right from the start, the better equipped he is as a competitor, and the less likely he is to make mistakes. And mistakes cost ballgames.

But this book is not only for the player. It is also for the football fan. By becoming more familiar with the rules and particularly with the official's signals, the spectator in the stands and the spectator at home before his TV screen can better understand what is going on and why. The spectator's enjoyment of the game increases with his knowledge.

Rules were created and are enforced to insure fair play for both teams. Football wouldn't be a sport without them — it's essential that we know the rules and use them properly.

CLARY ANDERSON

Clary Anderson, presently the head football coach at Montclair State College, has been a successful coach for nearly four decades on both the high school and college levels. He has compiled one of the outstanding records in the country, having won more than 90 per cent of his games. He is the author of *Make the Team in Football.*

# RULE DIFFERENCES

The rules illustrated and interpreted in this book are fundamental and apply equally to high school, college, and professional football except where noted otherwise. In extracting the essential meaning and purpose of the key rules, the editors relied on a variety of codes, including those used by the National Collegiate Athletic Association, the National Federation of State High School Athletic Associations, and the National Football League.

In contrast to baseball, where the rules are virtually the same regardless of the level at which the sport is played, football has never achieved uniformity. The primary reasons for this are that football is a more rugged game with much greater physical contact and that football strategy and tactics are more complex. This is particularly true of the professional sport, whose players are more mature and possess greater physical skill, and whose officials are more mindful of putting on games that continue to be exciting and appeal to the general public. This combination accounts for football's changing nature.

The most recent example of a sweeping change in the rules occurred on April 25, 1974 when the NFL adopted a sudden-death overtime period for all its games, moved the goal posts back to the end line, and made other changes to "open up" the passing attack and aid kickoff and punt returns.

Unlike high schools and colleges, which have never had an overtime rule, the professionals have had one since 1947 but solely for their playoff and championship games. The purpose in extending this rule to all pre-season and regular-season games, of course, is to reduce the number of tie results. The NFL decided to add one tie-break period of 15 minutes to each tie game. The team that scores first, whether by safety, field goal, or touchdown, wins. If neither team scores during the period, the game then ends officially as a tie. (In the playoffs and the Super Bowl, the teams will continue to play as many overtime periods as necessary until a score is made to break the tie.)

By positioning the goal posts 10 yards back from the goal line, to the end line of the end zone, the NFL reversed a rule that had been on the books for 41 years. The pros' thinking in 1933 was that moving the goal posts up to the goal line would increase the opportunities to score field goals. And it certainly did! In the last decade especially, as the kicking specialists became ever more proficient, the numerous field goals cheapened the value of the touchdown. (Incidentally, the college authorities, who originally had the goal posts on the goal line, moved them back in 1927 to the end line, where they have remained ever since. The reason for their move was concern for the players' safety. It was more unlikely that players would collide with the posts at the end line position.)

The NFL, however, is retaining the length of the crossbar between the uprights at 18 feet 6 inches while the colleges will still use a crossbar nearly 5 feet longer, with uprights 23 feet 4 inches apart.

The NFL also decided that the field-goal attempt should be made more of a gamble by requiring that the ball be returned to the line of scrimmage or the 20-yard line, whichever is farther from the goal line, in the event of a missed kick. Previously, it cost a team nothing to try for a long field goal instead of punting because if the 3-point attempt missed, the opposing team took possession on its own 20-yard line. With the new ruling, a team will think twice before attempting a long field goal and risk turning the ball over to their opponents in favorable field position.

Passing, notably the long touchdown "bombs," had been made more difficult in recent seasons by the harassing and "bumping" tactics of the defenders against the receivers. To counter this somewhat, the NFL determined that a receiver cannot be knocked out of a play by a block below the waist—the "roll" or cross-body block—and once he is 3 yards past the line of scrimmage, he can be hit or "bumped" only once by a defensive player. The penalty for holding by an offensive player, common in pass-blocking situations, was lessened from 15 yards to 10 yards.

To promote more and longer kickoff returns, the NFL pushed the kickoff line back from the kicking team's 40-yard line to the 35, while punt returns are encouraged by the new rule that players on the kicking team cannot cross the line of scrimmage until the ball is kicked.

Through the years an important source of difference has been the substitution rule, with the pros proving more consistent in this respect than the collegians. After employing the free-substitution rule from 1943 to 1945 because of wartime conditions, the pros adopted the rule—popularly known as the two-platoon rule—permanently in 1950. It allows the teams to substitute without restriction at any time except when the ball is actually in play.

Many observers credit the increasing popularity of professional football to this rule. It has made possible the use of offensive and defensive platoons, enabling players to concentrate their skills on the phase of the game in which they excel. Teams can also compete at full speed since each platoon can rest on the bench when the other platoon is in action. The art of specialization has been refined to such an extent that special platoons go in for specific action, such as the kick-off or the punt.

Another difference in the rules is scoring the try-for-point after a touchdown. In an attempt to reduce the number of tie games, colleges adopted a two-point rule. If the ball is carried or passed successfully over the goal line — in the same manner as scoring a touchdown — the try counts for 2 points. If the team elects to place-kick (convert) the try, then it is worth only 1 point.

Most high schools follow the college rule while the other schools and the National Football League have continued with the old rule crediting only 1 point whether the successful try is a kick, run or pass.

The colleges also spot the ball for the try after touchdown on the 3-yard line while high schools and the professionals spot the ball on the 2-yard line.

On running plays, the colleges and high schools differ from the pros as to whether the runner may continue after he slips or falls to the ground without being tackled. The professionals permit the runner to continue — even though his knee, for example, may have touched the ground — so long as contact has not been made by a defensive player. The runner may not advance, under college and high school rules, after any part of his body except his hands and feet touches the ground.

A last basic difference concerns the recovery of fumbles. All three sets of rules permit any player from either team to advance with a fumble if the ball is caught in the air. When the fumble has touched the ground, the college rule states that only the team that has fumbled can advance the ball. The opposing team can only recover it. Under professional and high school rules a fumble may be picked up and advanced by any player on either team.

7

# DEFINITIONS OF TERMS

**Batting:** Striking the ball intentionally with a hand or arm. It is permissible for any player eligible to touch a forward pass to bat the ball while the pass is in the air. It is also permissible to bat the ball if the player is blocking a punt. In other cases of a free ball, batting is illegal. The penalty is 15 yards.

**Blocker:** A player using his body to obstruct an opponent. An offensive blocker must observe the restrictions on the use of hands and arms.

**Clipping:** A type of block in which the player runs or dives into the back or the back of the legs of an opponent other than the runner. Clipping is legal in line play if it done in a rectangular area which is 4 yards wide on each side of the middle offensive lineman and 3 yards deep on either side of the scrimmage line. In the open field clipping is illegal. The penalty is 15 yards from the spot of the foul.

**Crawling:** An attempt by the runner to advance the ball after he has been tackled. The penalty is 5 yards.

**Delay of Game:** Any failure by a team to be ready for play within the specified time limit or any action that prolongs the game. The penalty is 5 yards.

**Double Foul:** When both teams commit fouls and the penalties offset each other.

**Down:** The unit of play. When a team has first down, it has four plays, or downs, in which to gain 10 yards to retain possession of the ball. If the first down is within the opponent's 10-yard line, then the team has four downs to gain the remaining distance to the goal line.

**Fair Catch:** A receiver of a kick signals for a fair catch by raising one arm directly above his head. He then is protected against being tackled when he makes the catch but gives up his right to advance the ball.

**Field Goal:** The ball is place-kicked or drop-kicked from scrimmage over the opposing team's crossbar. The kick scores 3 points.

**Forward Pass:** A pass thrown on a scrimmage play toward the opponent's goal line. Only the offensive team may throw a forward pass, and it must be thrown in or behind the neutral zone.

**Foul:** Any infraction of the rules that will draw a penalty.

**Free Ball:** A live ball in play, except for a forward pass, that is not in possession of a player.

**Fumble:** When a player loses possession of the ball, except when he passes, kicks or hands the ball off.

8

**Goal Line:** The line that has to be reached or crossed by the team in possession of the ball in order to score a touchdown. The goal lines separate the end zones from the 100-yard field of play.

**Half:** The game is divided into two halves, each half is divided into two periods, or quarters. The half is started with a kick-off. Playing time of a half is 30 minutes in College and Professional football, 24 minutes in High School. Teams may leave the field at the end of the first half. Halftime intermission is 15 minutes in High School and College games, 20 minutes in Professional football.

**Huddle:** Players get together in a group, usually forming a circle, to decide on the strategy and the signals for the next play. The huddle is not limited to the offensive team. The defensive team may also huddle to determine what strategy to follow.

**Hurdling:** The runner jumps over or attempts to jump over a player who is on his feet in the open field. At the scrimmage line, hurdling is defined as jumping over a player with both feet or both knees foremost. It is illegal and the penalty is 15 yards.

**Interception:** The catching of any pass by an opponent who is then allowed to run with the ball.

**Kicking:** a) Drop-kick: The kicker drops the ball and kicks it just as it touches or rises from the ground.

b) Kick-off: The ball is put into play by a place-kick, drop-kick, or with the use of a tee, at the start of the game, the start of the second half, after a field goal or try-for-point after a touchdown. The kick-off takes place from the 40-yard line of the kicking team.

c) Place-kick: The ball is held for the kicker by a teammate.

d) Punt: The ball is kicked before it touches the ground on a scrimmage play or as a free kick after a safety is scored.

e) Return-kick: A kick made by a player immediately after catching a kick; it is now seldom used.

**Lateral:** This is also known as a backward pass. Any player may pass the ball backward or parallel to his goal line to a teammate at any time.

**Line-to-gain:** The yard line 10 yards in advance of the most forward point of the ball that the team must reach in four downs or lose possession of the ball.

**Man-in-motion:** One player of the offensive backfield may be in motion before and as the ball is snapped, but he must be moving away from or parallel to the defensive team's goal line. In high school, if the back starts from the scrimmage line, he must stop for one second before going in motion and must be 5 yards in back of the line when the ball is snapped. The pro rule requires the man in motion to start at least 1 yard in back of the scrimmage line. If he is illegally in motion, the penalty is 5 yards.

**Multiple Foul:** When two or more fouls are committed by a team, the opposing team has a choice of penalties.

**Neutral Zone:** An area the length of the football that is between the offensive and defensive scrimmage lines.

**Offside:** When any part of the player's body is beyond his scrimmage line, or his restraining line before the ball is in play.

**Out-of-bounds:** The area outside the sidelines and endlines including the lines. The ball or a player touching the sideline or endline is considered out-of-bounds.

**Period:** The total time of the game is divided into four quarters, or periods. In College and Professional football each period lasts 15 minutes; in High School games it is 12 minutes long. Two periods make a half. Play in the first and third period begins with a kick-off. The second and fourth periods start after an exchange of goals, but play is resumed from the point where it was stopped by the end of the previous period. Before the second and fourth periods there is an intermission of one or two minutes, but players are not permitted to leave the field.

**Recovering:** Gaining possession of the ball after a fumble.

**Runner:** Player who is in possession of the ball.

**Safety:** Two points scored by the team not in possession of the ball. Among the ways a safety is scored are: the runner is tackled in his end zone or goes out-of-bounds from the end zone; the offensive team fumbles the ball out-of-bounds from the end zone; the snap from center goes out of the end zone, and the defensive team is responsible for the ball becoming dead in the offensive team's end zone, with the ball still in possession of the offensive team.

**Scrimmage:** The action that results when a play starts with the center snapping the ball back and ends when the ball is dead.

**Scrimmage Line:** The imaginary line established for each team by the point of the ball nearest its goal line. The offensive team must have at least 7 players on or within a foot of the scrimmage line. Defensive players may be positioned anywhere behind their scrimmage line.

**Shift:** When two or more players of the offensive team change position after lining up and before the ball is snapped. After a shift, all offensive players must remain stationary for a second before the snap.

**Snap:** When the center passes or hands the ball back to a backfield player. Also known as centering the ball.

**Tackle:** The maneuver by which a defensive player stops the runner by using his hands, arms or body.

**Time-out:**  When play is stopped at the request of either team for a period of 1½ minutes. The time-out may be of longer duration when necessary, such as when medical attention is given to an injured player. The referee also may call timeouts at his discretion.

**Touchback:**  When the offensive team is responsible for putting the ball in the defensive team's end zone while giving up possession of the ball on such plays as the kick-off or punt. After a touchback, the team with the ball starts the next play with a first down on its 20-yard-line.

**Touchdown:**   Six points are scored when a player in possession of the ball reaches the goal line or is in the end zone of the opposing team by running, catching a pass or recovering a fumble.

**Try-for-point:**   The play that follows a touchdown even if time has run out in a period. The team scoring the touchdown has one play from scrimmage in which to run or pass the ball over the goal line or to place or drop-kick the ball over the crossbar. In High School, College and Professional play, a successful kick scores 1 point. In College and most High School games, a successful run or pass scores 2 points. In the National Football League and some High School games, a successful run or pass scores 1 point.

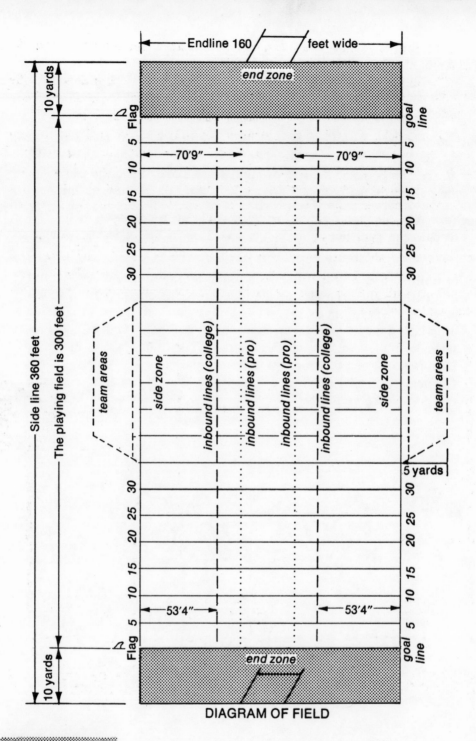

**DIAGRAM OF FIELD**

## THE FIELD

The playing field is 360 feet long and 160 feet wide. When the dimensions are given in yards, the rectangular field is 120 yards long by 53⅓ yards wide. The *goal lines* are 300 feet (100 yards) apart. At each end of the field there is an *end zone*, 30 feet (10 yards) deep. The goal lines, which are located within the end zones, and the end zones are the area in which touchdowns and safeties are scored.

The field is marked every 5 yards by a distinct line running across the width of the field from sideline to sideline.

The entire playing field is bordered by a solid line. The area within the sidelines and the endlines is *inbounds*. The sidelines and the endlines themselves, as well as the area beyond these lines, are *out-of-bounds*.

On the field, parallel to the sidelines and running from goal line to goal line, are two *inbounds lines*. These divide the field into three equal parts, each 53 feet, 4 inches wide. In Professional football the inbounds lines are 70 feet 9 inches from the sidelines. When a play ends out-of-bounds or in a *side zone* (between the sideline and the inbounds line), the ball is placed at the nearer inbounds line for the next play.

The teams have a place on opposite sides of the field for a players' bench, coaches and other authorized personnel. These are called *team areas* and are located between the 35-yard lines. They are 5 to 6 feet from the sidelines.

Flags with flexible staffs are placed at each corner formed by the goal line and a sideline.

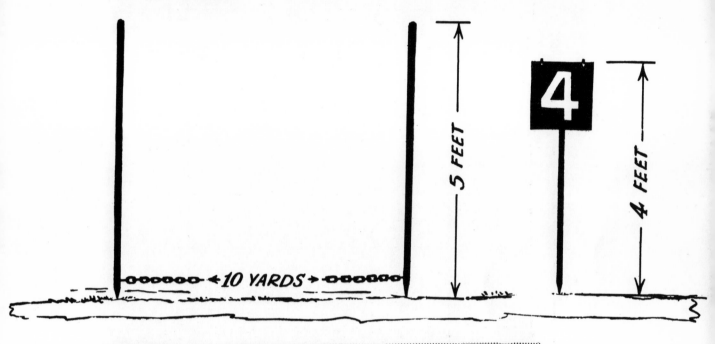

## YARDAGE CHAIN AND DOWN MARKER

The *yardage chain* is exactly 10 yards long when fully extended. It is joined to two rods, each at least 5 feet high. It is used to measure if the offensive team has *gained* at least *10 yards* in *four downs* (plays) or less. When at least 10 yards has been gained, the offensive team has made a *first down* and has four downs again in which to gain another 10 yards.

The *down indicator* is on a rod that is at least 4 feet high and holds four "cards" lettered 1, 2, 3 and 4. The indicator marks the most forward point of the ball at the *start of each down* and the "card" indicating the number of the down is displayed.

# THE GOAL POSTS

The *goal posts* are located on the end lines. The posts are 18 feet, 6 inches apart in both High School and Professional football. Posts in College games are placed 23 feet, 4 inches apart. In all cases, the *crossbar* is placed 10 feet above the ground. Professional rules require that the goal posts must be *padded* with kapok or foam rubber. "Offset" posts, set behind the end line but with the crossbar extended to the end line, are used in Professional football.

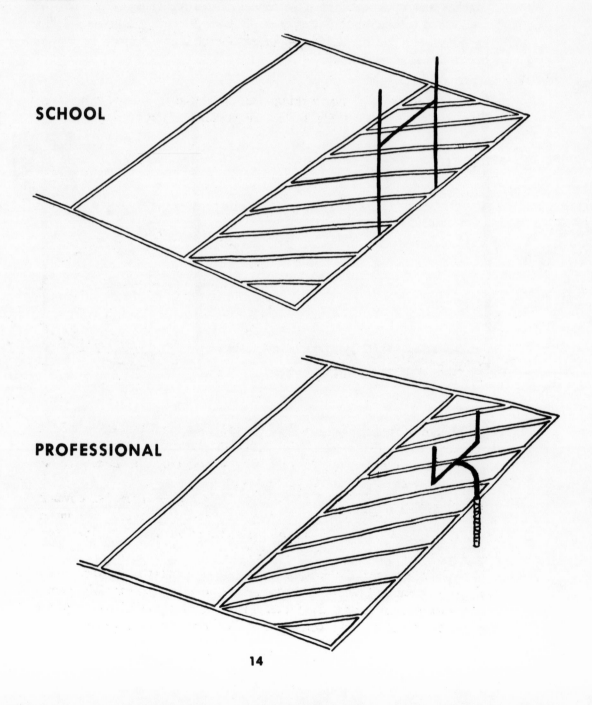

SCHOOL

PROFESSIONAL

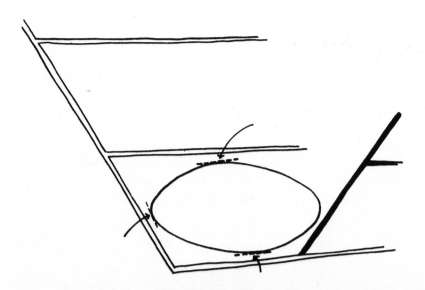

Under College rules, no markings may be placed in the end zones that are closer than 2 feet to the goal line, the endlines or the sidelines.

## THE FOOTBALL

The football must weigh between 14 and 15 ounces. It is to be inflated to an air pressure of between 12½ and 13½ pounds. The *long circumference* must measure between 28 and 28½ inches. The *short circumference* must be between 21¼ and 21½ inches.

In High School games, the football used, either rubber- or leather-covered, should be of a natural tan color with white 1-inch stripes, 3 to 3½ inches from each end of the football to the near edge of the stripe. Another color may be used with the approval of both teams.

In College games, the football should be of a natural tan color, but a white or colored ball, with or without stripes, may be used for night games.

In Professional games, the football is to be of a natural tan color for day games and of a brown color with white stripes for night games.

# STANDARD NUMBERING SYSTEM

To help identify players by position, a *standard numbering system* is *recommended* for High Schools and Colleges. The numbers assigned for *ends* are 80 to 89; for *tackles,* 70 to 79; for *guards,* 60 to 69; for *centers,* 50 to 59; and for *backs,* 1 to 49.

While this numbering system is only *recommended* for High Schools and Colleges, Professional football has *required* standard numbering for many years. Starting with the 1973 season, NFL players are numbered as follows: *quarterbacks* and *kickers,* 1 to 19; all *running* and *defensive backs,* 20 to 49; *centers* and *linebackers,* 50 to 59; *defensive linemen* and *interior offensive linemen* (except for *centers*), 60 to 79, and *wide receivers* and *tight ends,* 80 to 89. (All players who were in the NFL prior to 1973 may use their old numbers.)

Regardless of his number, however, a player may play any position; in some cases the referee must be notified of the change of position.

# IMPROPER EQUIPMENT

A player will be ordered off the field by the official for an improper uniform. In this case, the number on the player's jersey is too small. *Numbers* must be at least *8 inches* high on the front of the jersey, and *10 inches* on the back.

This player will be ordered off the field and not allowed in the game until he has changed his jersey. Any equipment which, in the opinion of the officials, would confuse the opposing players is illegal.

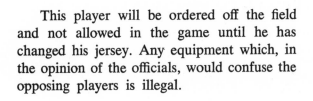

Jerseys or helmets that are similar in color to the football and tend to conceal it are forbidden. The use of camouflage of any sort is illegal and players will not be permitted on the field until the infraction of the rules is corrected.

This player, too, will be ordered off the field because he is too well protected. Players are not permitted to have leather, or other hard material, regardless of how well it is covered or padded, on hands, wrists, forearms or elbows.

17

Backfield stars have been described as being "slippery as an eel," but any material that helps them achieve such elusiveness is strictly forbidden. The use of oil, grease or any slippery substance on the player's uniform is illegal.

A player will not be allowed in the game if he wears a face mask with sharp edges. Face masks should be of non-breakable, molded plastic with rounded edges or with rubber-covered wire.

# OFFICIALS

White circles designate the offensive team; solid black squares show the defensive team. When the play starts at the scrimmage line, the officials take up the positions indicated on the diagram.

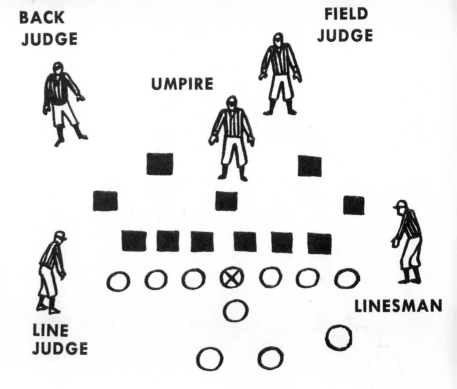

## THE REFEREE

The *referee* has over-all charge and control of the game. His decisions are final except in those matters specifically under the jurisdiction of other officials. Among his duties are spotting the ball where play is to resume, declaring the ball in play or dead, signalling infractions of rules and pacing off the penalties. He is the authority for the score.

### THE UMPIRE

The *umpire* has primary jurisdiction over the equipment and the conduct of the players. In each scrimmage he is particularly responsible for observing illegal play. He must also cover open play that develops after the linemen make their initial charge.

### THE LINESMAN

The *linesman* has primary jurisdiction over the neutral zone and infractions (called OFFSIDE) of the scrimmage formation. Under the supervision of the referee, he marks the progress of the ball and keeps an accurate count of the downs. Under his direction assistants operate the yardage chain to mark and hold the starting point and *line-to-gain* for each series of downs as well as the *down indicator*.

### THE LINE JUDGE

The *line judge* keeps time of game as a backup for the clock operator, and checks for offside, encroachment and other actions pertaining to the scrimmage line prior to or at the snap.

### THE FIELD JUDGE

The *field judge,* when there is no Back Judge, has primary jurisdiction over the timing of the game. He starts and stops the game clock and keeps the referee informed of the time remaining. He acts for the referee on downfield play.

### THE BACK JUDGE

In professional football, the *back judge* takes over the responsibility of timing the game and checks for infractions in his side zone.

The use of a Back Judge is *optional* in College football, but is *required* in Professional.

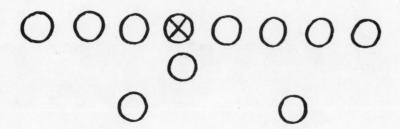

## SCRIMMAGE LINE

Count the number of players on the scrimmage line. One man too many? Not at all. An *eight-man line* may be a very rare sight in football, but there is nothing in the rules to make it illegal. This is also true of a nine-man line or a ten-man line. What the rules do require is that there be *at least seven men* on the scrimmage line in order for the formation to be legal. Paul Brown, the former head coach of the Cleveland Browns, once invented and used plays based on an eight-man line.

## ILLEGAL FORMATION

This five-man line is illegal under the rules since it does not meet the seven-man minimum required on the scrimmage line.

## LEGAL LEG LOCK

It is legal for the two *guards* and the *center* to line up and *lock legs*. The rules permit this, but only for the center and the guards. It is against the rules for other linemen to lock legs. This unusual way for players to line up is not used today for tactical reasons, not because the rules forbid it.

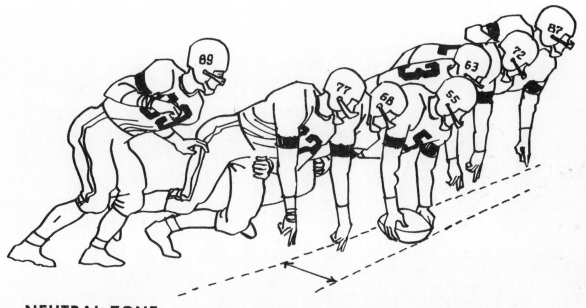

## NEUTRAL ZONE

Because one careless player (No. 68), has placed his hand too far forward, the team will draw an *offside* penalty. All linemen except the center are required to be behind their scrimmage line. Only the *center* is allowed to have any part of his body *in the neutral zone*. The neutral zone is measured by the *length of the football* and is the area between the offensive and defensive scrimmage lines. The center, however, is not permitted to be beyond the neutral zone. Should he place himself beyond the neutral zone, the team will draw an offside penalty.

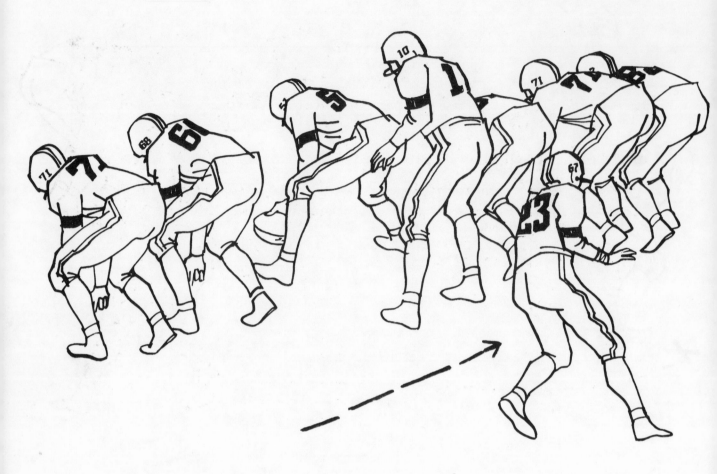

## MAN IN MOTION

As this backfield man (No. 23) goes into motion before the ball is snapped, all his teammates must remain stationary because only *one player* is allowed to be in motion. But he became careless as to the direction he is taking. He is moving toward the scrimmage line. In all cases, the man in motion should be traveling a path either parallel to or away from the scrimmage line. Otherwise, his team will be penalized 5 yards.

## END IN MOTION

This looks like the start of the old-fashioned end-around play. The end (No. 83) appears to be legally in motion because he is traveling a path backward from the line of scrimmage as the ball is about to be snapped. But the formation is illegal because, having started from the scrimmage line, he has left only six players on the line. The rule requires at least seven linemen. The penalty is 5 yards. It is important to remember that in properly executing one maneuver that infractions of other rules are not committed.

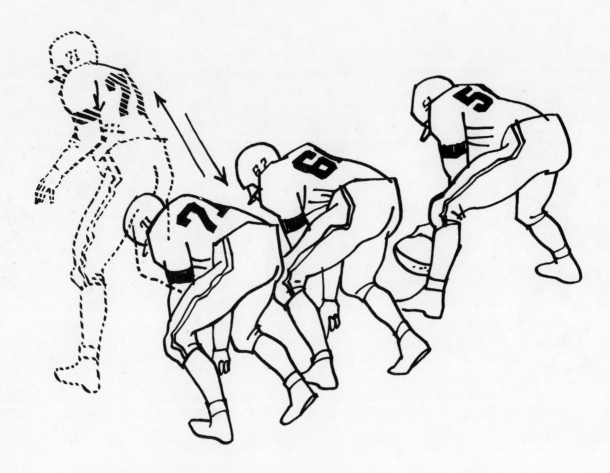

## RETURN BEFORE SNAP (Offensive)

An over-anxious lineman (No. 71) has "jumped" the signal and crossed the scrimmage line before the ball is snapped. He immediately recovers and returns to his set position, or three-point stance, without making contact with an opponent. The play still has not started but the lineman is declared to have made a false start. The rule is that once an offensive lineman has assumed a set position, he cannot charge or move in such a way as to lead an opposing player to think the ball is being snapped. The penalty is 5 yards.

## RETURN BEFORE SNAP (Defensive)

The defensive lineman (No. 75) has charged into the neutral zone and then has returned to his proper position behind the defensive scrimmage line. Since the ball has not been snapped and no contact was made with an opponent, he is not considered to be offside and there is no penalty. However, if the defensive lineman does this repeatedly after having been warned, he will be penalized 5 yards.

## OFFSETTING PENALTIES

If both the offensive and defensive linemen have charged before the ball is snapped, and the official rules that they did so *simultaneously*, then a double foul is called and the penalties offset each other. However, if it is ruled that the action of the offensive player caused his opponent to go offside, then the offensive team will be penalized 5 yards.

## OFFSETTING PENALTIES

The defensive lineman charges into his opponent before the ball is snapped. At the same time the center lifts the football off the ground. While the defensive team will be ruled offside, the center will be penalized for an illegal snap because he is allowed only one *continuous* motion to pass the ball back. Thus the penalties will offset each other.

# SNAPPING (CENTERING) THE BALL

Snapping (centering) the ball is the start of every play from scrimmage. If the center doesn't handle this part of the play properly, then the offensive team is in trouble. The center is expected not to raise either end of the ball more than 45 degrees before the snap. He must keep the football pointing toward the opponent's goal line. He must hand or pass the ball back in one continuous motion and is not permitted to fake a snap.

# ADVANCING THE BALL

At any time, it is legal for the man with the ball (No. 28) to hand it backward or to pass it backward or to the side (lateral) to a teammate.

28

## HANDING BALL FORWARD

The football may be handed forward from one back (No. 17) to another (No. 21) during scrimmage play, but only if *both backs* are *behind the scrimmage line*. If the backs are beyond the scrimmage line, such action is illegal.

## HAND-OFF TO LINEMAN

The only occasion on which a lineman is allowed to receive a forward hand-off is illustrated by No. 67. He has turned around so that he faces his own goal line and is at least 1 yard behind the scrimmage line.

## THE STIFF-ARM

The ball-carrier (or runner) is employing a standard technique — the stiff arm — to prevent an opponent from tackling him. The ball-carrier is permitted to use his hand or an arm to push away an opponent.

## ILLEGAL HELP TO RUNNER

A teammate is trying to help the ball-carrier gain a few more yards. This is illegal and the team will receive a 15-yard penalty. Members of the offensive team are not allowed to push, lift or otherwise assist the runner directly.

## BLOCKING

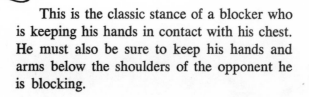

A legal shoulder block is being completed upon No. 79. The rule states that a blocker is not permitted to use his hands or arms.

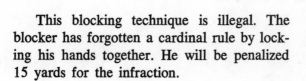

This is the classic stance of a blocker who is keeping his hands in contact with his chest. He must also be sure to keep his hands and arms below the shoulders of the opponent he is blocking.

This blocking technique is illegal. The blocker has forgotten a cardinal rule by locking his hands together. He will be penalized 15 yards for the infraction.

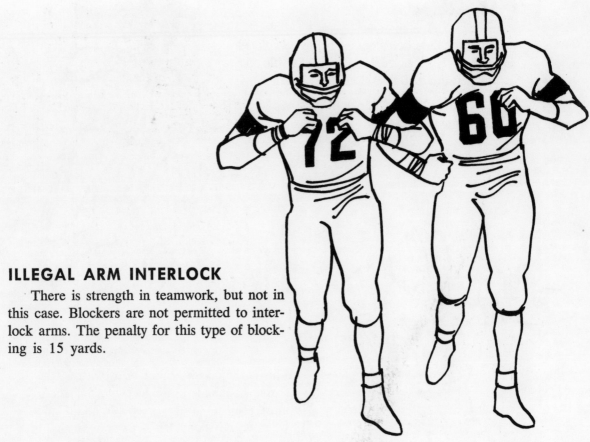

## ILLEGAL ARM INTERLOCK

There is strength in teamwork, but not in this case. Blockers are not permitted to interlock arms. The penalty for this type of blocking is 15 yards.

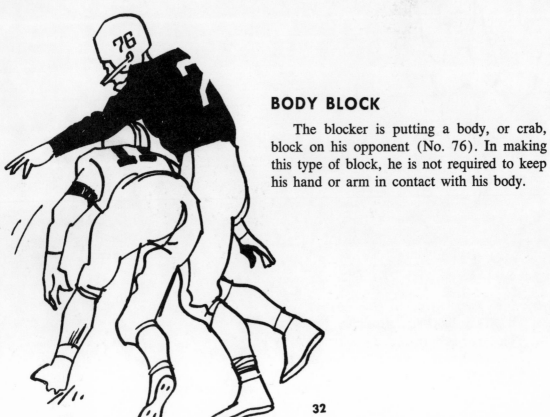

## BODY BLOCK

The blocker is putting a body, or crab, block on his opponent (No. 76). In making this type of block, he is not required to keep his hand or arm in contact with his body.

## USE OF HANDS

The offensive player (No. 77) is trying to push his opponent (No. 68) with his hands. Such action is in violation of the rule and is punished by a 15-yard penalty. *No blocker is allowed to use his hands to push, pull or grab an opposing player.*

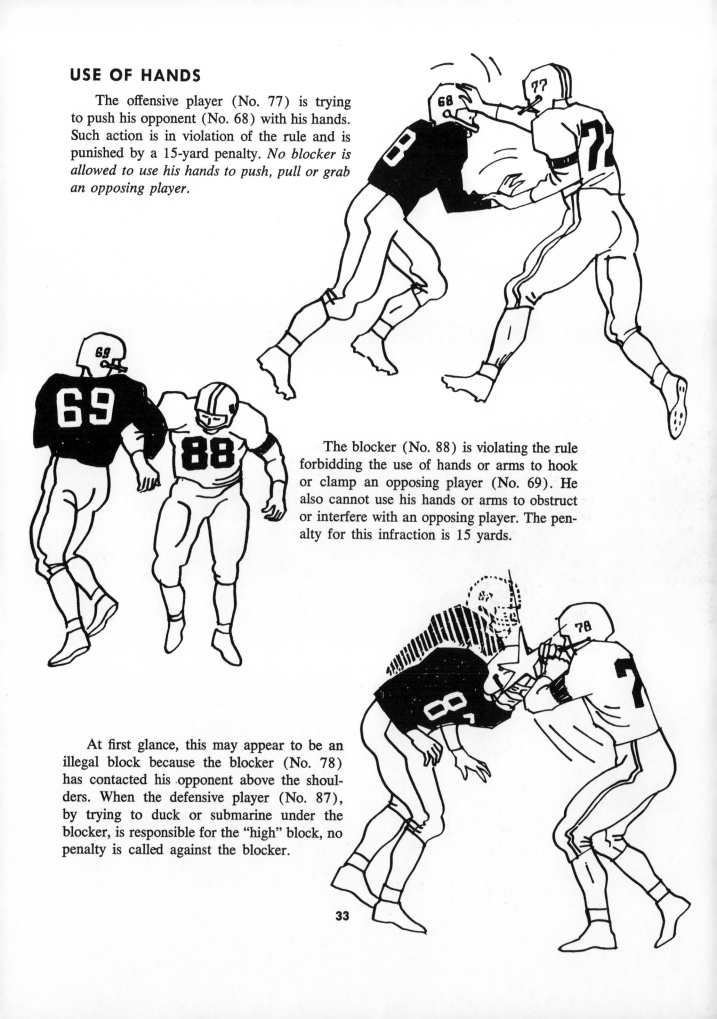

The blocker (No. 88) is violating the rule forbidding the use of hands or arms to hook or clamp an opposing player (No. 69). He also cannot use his hands or arms to obstruct or interfere with an opposing player. The penalty for this infraction is 15 yards.

At first glance, this may appear to be an illegal block because the blocker (No. 78) has contacted his opponent above the shoulders. When the defensive player (No. 87), by trying to duck or submarine under the blocker, is responsible for the "high" block, no penalty is called against the blocker.

33

# TACKLING

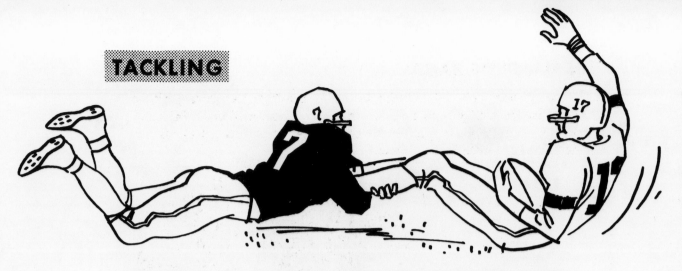

The defender (No. 7) is making the standard two-armed tackle to bring the runner (No. 17) down. As soon as any part of the runner's body, except his hands and feet, touches the ground, he is not permitted to make any further advance. In High School and College rules a runner is "down" whether he has touched the ground because of a tackle or simply through slipping or falling. In Professional football, when a runner slips or falls he is not considered "down" and may continue to advance the ball until he is tackled.

This may not be the classic way to make a tackle, but it is *legal to grab the runner* around the neck or any part of his body. The tackler, however, has to be sure that he is not grabbing the runner's face mask.

A push in time may stop a long gain and the defender (No. 88) is within the rules when he pushes the runner (No. 25) to the ground. The defense is allowed to use hands and arms to tackle, push, shove or otherwise *throw the runner* to the ground.

## LEGAL USE OF HANDS

The defender (No. 78) is using his hands in a legal manner to push the blocker and pursue the runner. A *defensive player* is allowed to use his hands and arms to grasp, push, pull or lift other offensive players out of his way if he is trying to reach the runner.

## DISQUALIFYING FOUL

The defensive player (No. 70) will be disqualified for *punching* his opponent (No. 15) and his team will be penalized 15 yards. The rule forbids any player from striking another with his fist, forearm, elbow or locked hands, or to kick or knee an opponent. The *disqualifying foul* rule differs from the *personal foul* rule in that the action is considered by the officials to be performed deliberately and willfully with intent to harm.

## PERSONAL FOULS

### KNEEING

The blocker (No. 76) is guilty of *kneeing* his opponent (No. 15) and is penalized 15 yards since it is not considered a deliberate act. Under the same rule no player shall hit an opponent either on the head, neck or face with the heel, back or side of the hand or with the wrist.

### ACCIDENTAL KICK

No. 47 has *inadvertently kicked* an opposing player on the ground while trying to reach the runner. He will be penalized 15 yards under the rule that prohibits any player from swinging his foot and striking another player above the knee with his foot.

## TRIPPING

The runner (No. 12) is being tripped by the defensive player (No. 17) and the infraction will cost the team on defense 15 yards *Tripping* is never allowed, regardless of whether the tripped player is carrying the ball or not.

## PILING ON

Since the runner is already on the ground, the defensive player (No. 19) who is about to fall on him will be guilty of *piling on* and will be penalized 15 yards. Once the ball becomes dead players are expected to stop running into or throwing themselves on an opponent.

Any hurdling by the runner (No. 11) is best left for the track event. He will be penalized 15 yards for jumping over an opponent at the scrimmage line.

When the runner (No. 12) is obviously out of bounds, no defensive player may tackle him. The penalty is 15 yards.

## CLIPPING

The block being performed on No. 69 is called *clipping* and, contrary to popular belief, it is *not necessarily illegal*. Clipping means a player has thrown himself across the back of the legs or the back of an opponent other than the runner. In a scrimmage play clipping is permitted in an area about 6 yards in depth and 4 yards wide on each side of the middle lineman. But any offensive player outside this area who is in motion toward the ball when it is snapped may not clip in this area. During a kick-off, or other free-kick down, no clipping is permitted. The penalty is 15 yards.

The referee has already taken possession of the ball, making it clear the play is over. The illegal tackle will draw a 15-yard penalty under the rule that bars any player from running into or making contact with an opponent obviously out of the play either before or after the ball is dead.

The face mask or protector is off-limits and grabbing a player's mask is forbidden. The penalty is 15 yards.

## FORWARD PASS

### ILLEGAL PASS

The passer (No. 21), has gone one step too far before throwing the ball because his left foot has *crossed the neutral zone*. It is is 5 yards from the spot of the pass and the down counts.

### LEGAL PASS

The passer is now able to throw the ball legally even though he has stepped past his own scrimmage line. He has been careful not to go beyond the neutral zone.

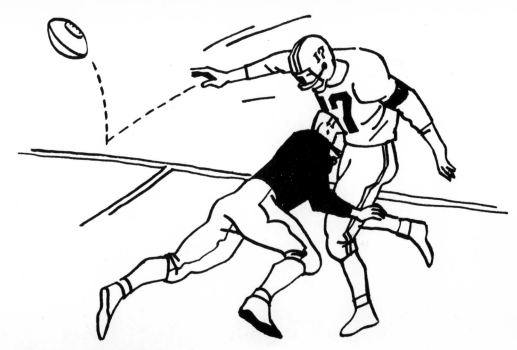

## INTENTIONAL GROUNDING

The passer will be penalized for throwing the ball away to prevent loss of yardage. He is about to be tackled and brought down. Since there is no receiver reasonably near the area, the passer is guilty of *intentionally grounding the pass*. The penalty is loss of 15 yards and a down.

## JUDGMENT CALL

This passing situation is more complicated. The passer, No. 11, throws the ball in the general direction of the receiver just as he is about to be tackled. The question that the referee has to settle is whether it was a bona-fide attempt at completing a pass or whether it was a clever attempt to prevent a loss on the play. This is a judgment call and, unless the evidence is overwhelming on the other side, the official will rule it a legal forward pass.

## ELIGIBLE RECEIVERS

The arrows point to the only players on the offensive team who are eligible pass receivers: the two ends on the scrimmage line and the players in the backfield who are at least 1 yard in back of the scrimmage line. In Professional football, the T quarterback is not an eligible receiver. The rule on eligible receivers remains the same regardless of whether the end man is a tackle or guard in another formation. All 11 players on the defensive team are eligible to intercept a pass.

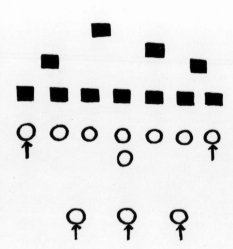

## STEPPING OUT-OF-BOUNDS

In the illustration at the left, an otherwise eligible receiver has made himself ineligible by going out-of-bounds before returning to the field to catch a pass. On the right, the ineligible receiver becomes eligible because the pass has been touched by a defensive player.

## LANDING OUT-OF-BOUNDS

The receiver, No. 21, made a nice catch of the forward pass, but the effort was wasted. Though he is inbounds when he leaped for the ball, he landed outside the sideline. In such a situation the receiver is ruled out-of-bounds and the pass is incomplete.

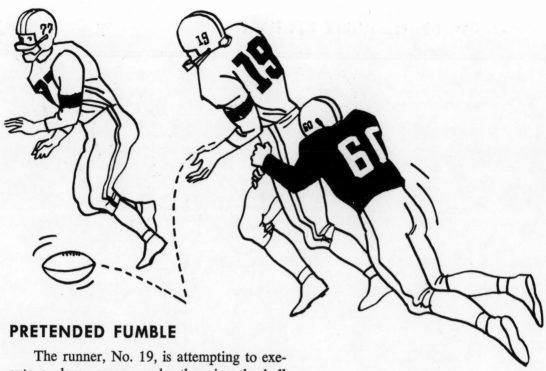

## PRETENDED FUMBLE

The runner, No. 19, is attempting to execute a clever maneuver by throwing the ball forward, pretending to fumble so that teammate No. 77 will recover the ball for additional yardage. But any attempt to throw the ball forward beyond the neutral zone is classified as an illegal forward pass and will be penalized 5 yards from that point.

## SIMULTANEOUS CATCH

In this example "half a loaf" is about as good as a whole one. The intended receiver (No. 89) and the defender (No. 21) caught the pass simultaneously. It will be ruled a completed pass and the ball given to the passing team. There is a limitation in such a situation: the receiver may not advance the ball.

## TOUCHING INELIGIBLE RECEIVER

The passing team may appear to be lucky because the football has bounced off the helmet of one of its players (No. 68) into the hands of another. But it will not be ruled a completed forward pass because the ball, even if only accidentally, touched an ineligible receiver first.

## JUDGMENT CALL

The receiver caught the forward pass, or did he? He has possession of the ball momentarily. It slipped through his hands just as he was about to take his first step. *The judgment of the nearest official* will determine whether the receiver actually had possession of the ball or whether the ruling should be an incomplete pass.

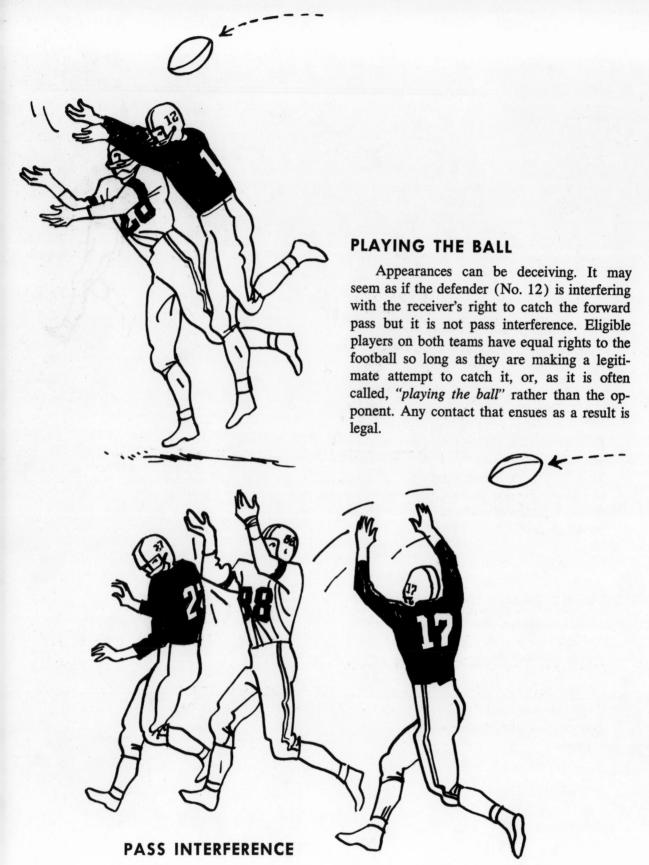

## PLAYING THE BALL

Appearances can be deceiving. It may seem as if the defender (No. 12) is interfering with the receiver's right to catch the forward pass but it is not pass interference. Eligible players on both teams have equal rights to the football so long as they are making a legitimate attempt to catch it, or, as it is often called, *"playing the ball"* rather than the opponent. Any contact that ensues as a result is legal.

## PASS INTERFERENCE

This is pass interference even though the offender (No. 17) has not made contact with the receiver (No. 88). No. 17 is attempting to distract the receiver from catching the pass by waving his arms in front of him. With his back to the play, the defender is not making an honest effort to "play the ball." Under the rule it is the passing team's ball at the spot of the foul.

## BEFORE THE PASS IS THROWN

The defender (No. 17) is not guilty of pass interference because contact with the receiver (No. 89) was made before the ball was thrown and was beyond the scrimmage line.

## INELIGIBLE RECEIVER DOWNFIELD

Offensive guard (No. 69), having completed his primary block on the opposing defensive player, is running downfield to assist with the blocking for the intended receiver. He is, however, committing an infraction of the rules: once he has lost contact with his opponent he cannot make a move downfield until the pass is thrown. He is not an eligible receiver and should not be downfield. The team will be penalized 10 yards for having an ineligible receiver downfield.

## PASS INTERFERENCE RULE

Even though the pass thrown by No. 17 has not yet crossed the scrimmage line, pass interference rules are in effect. The rules apply from *the moment the pass is thrown*. The defensive player (No. 25) is guilty of interfering with the intended pass receiver (No. 89) and the penalty will give the passing team a first down at the spot where the interference occurred.

## ALMOST A SAFETY

The defensive player (No. 78) has almost scored 2 points for his team by batting back a forward pass thrown from the end zone. If he had been *inside the end zone* instead of a few yards out when he batted back the pass, he would have been credited with a safety.

## DEAD BALL

The *ball is ruled dead* the instant a forward pass hits a goal post, even though it may bounce off and be caught by a player before it touches the ground. The rules state that the ball is dead upon hitting the goal posts, the crossbar, the ground or going out of bounds.

## FUMBLE ON A PASS PLAY

The passer (No. 12) has fumbled the ball in attempting to pass it forward to an eligible receiver (No. 27) behind the scrimmage line. It is ruled a fumble and not an incomplete pass. The importance of this is that now the defensive team can recover the ball. If it were an incomplete pass the passing team would automatically retain possession of the ball.

## INTERCEPTION

The pass has touched an ineligible receiver and the defender (No. 89) is about to intercept. The ruling is that *the interception stands* unless the defensive team prefers to take the penalty. A forward pass remains in play *only for an interception after touching an ineligible receiver.* In Professional football there is a penalty for intentional touching, none for accidental.

## SCHOOL AND PRO RULE

Two *eligible receivers* have caught the pass simultaneously. In High School and College it is ruled a completed pass, but among the Professionals it is ruled incomplete.

## BATTING BALL ON A PASS PLAY

The defender (No. 21) bats the attempted forward pass away from the intended receiver (No. 27). Under the rule the *defense* is allowed to bat the pass in any direction and at any time but the *offense* is allowed only to bat the ball to prevent an interception.

# KICKING

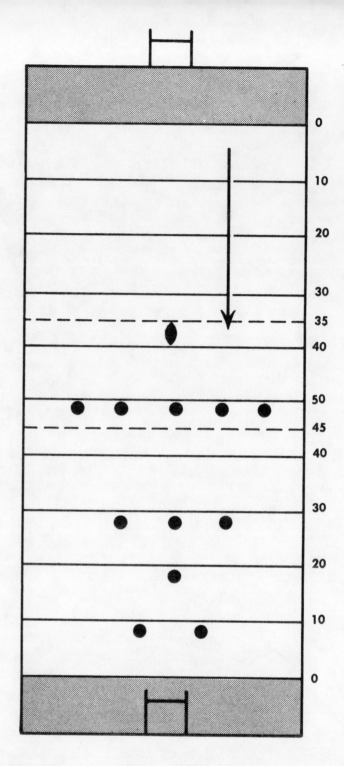

## KICK-OFF FORMATION

Five players of the *team receiving* the kick-off must be in an area 10 to 15 yards from the kick-off, between the 50-yard line and their own 45-yard line. There are no restrictions on where the other players are located, except that they must be in back of the first five players.

*Note: In the NFL, the kick-off is made from the 35-yard line.*

56

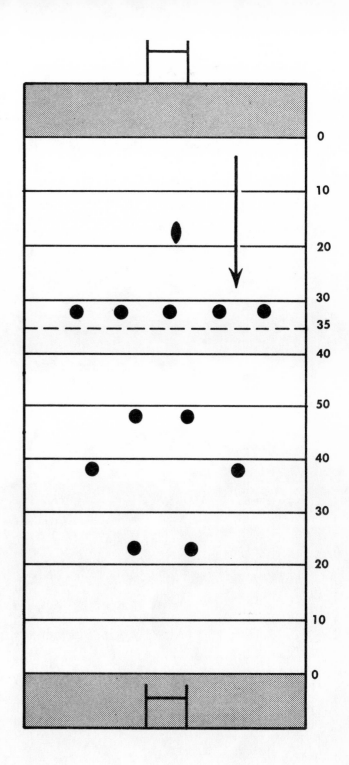

## FREE-KICK FORMATION

The free kick follows a safety. Five players of the *team receiving* the kick must be in an area 10 to 15 yards from the ball, between the 30-yard line and the 35-yard line.

## KICK-OFF

The ball is put into play at the start of each half by the *kick-off*. The ball is placed on the 40-yard line of the kicking team, usually resting on a tee, but a place-kick or a drop-kick may be used legally. The kick-off is also used to put the ball in play after a field goal or try-for-point after a touchdown.

## PUNT

The punt is usually used on a scrimmage play. The ball is kicked before it touches the ground. It may also be used as a free-kick after a safety. Team punting gives up possession of the ball.

## PLACE-KICK

The ball is held for the kicker by a teammate. The place-kick is used to score a field-goal, point-after-touchdown, and sometimes on a kick-off.

## DROP-KICK

The kicker drops the ball and kicks it just at the instant it touches the ground or a fraction of a second later. Seldom employed today, it can be used instead of the place-kick.

## ILLEGALLY KICKING THE BALL

The ball may not be kicked by any player except during a specific kicking play. Since the defensive player (No. 12) has deliberately kicked a free ball, the offensive team has possession of the ball at the spot where the rule infraction occurred. If the player on offense kicks the ball, his team is given a 15-yard penalty from the starting point of the play.

## ROUGHING THE KICKER

After the punter (No. 27) kicks the ball, an opposing player crashes into him: a clear violation of roughing-the-kicker regulations. The purpose of the rule is to protect the kicker and the holder of a place-kick during a scrimmage kick because they are vulnerable to contact. To gain protection under the rules, it has to be reasonably obvious that a kick will be made. Penalty for roughing the kicker is 15 yards.

## ON A BLOCKED PUNT

A roughing-the-kicker penalty will not be called on this play because *the punt has been blocked*. Such contact is considered a legitimate play when the punt is blocked. The defensive player (No. 77), therefore, is not violating any rules by running into the kicker.

## SLIGHT CONTACT

When the contact is slight, the defensive player (No. 77) will not be called for roughing the kicker.

## ON THE QUICK KICK

Since a *quick kick* was attempted, the defensive player (No. 70) is exempt from the roughing-the-kicker rule because it was not reasonably obvious that a scrimmage kick was planned. No penalty.

## FUMBLE ON KICKING PLAY   A fumble before the kick is attempted also exempts

the defensive players  from  the  roughing-the-kicker rule.

**WRONG**                    **RIGHT**

## FAIR CATCH SIGNAL

If the signal for a *fair catch* is given improperly, the receiving team is penalized 5 yards from the spot of the foul. On the left, the wrong way to signal; on the right, the player gives the proper signal.

## PROTECTING PUNT RECEIVER

The players crowd about the man catching the ball but they have to be careful to give him an *unmolested opportunity* to catch it. If they interfere, the penalty is 15 yards.

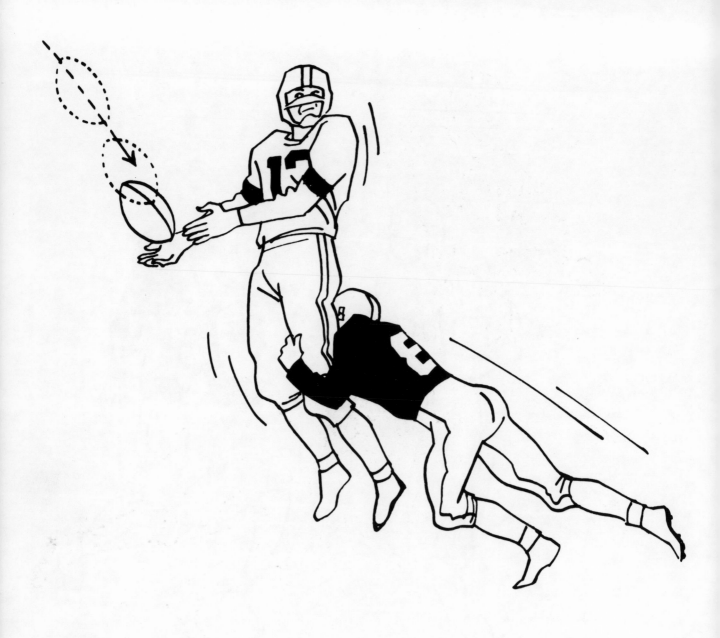

## ILLEGAL INTERFERENCE ON A CATCH

Even though he manages to catch the ball as he is being tackled, his team will be awarded a 15-yard penalty. Under the rule, illegal interference is called when a player is tackled before or when the ball arrives.

## NO FUMBLE ON CATCH

Although the receiver of the punt fumbled while he was being tackled, the official will rule no fumble. His opponent will be penalized 15 yards. The receiving team will retain possession of the ball because of the illegal interference.

## FAIR TACKLE

The receiver of the punt has fumbled and then is tackled by an opponent. No interference will be called. Protection against interference with the opportunity to catch a kick ends when the player *touches the ball*, except when it is a fair catch.

## TWO-STEP LIMIT

After making a fair catch, a player is allowed to take only two steps. The ball becomes dead at the spot where he caught it. If he tries to advance, he will be penalized 5 yards.

# OFFICIAL'S CODE OF SIGNALS

**OFFSIDE.** A player on either team has crossed his scrimmage line before the ball has been snapped (put into play). Penalty: 5 yards.

**ILLEGAL RETURN.** Return of a substitute previously disqualified, or before a down has been completed (College). Penalty: 15 yards.

**CLIPPING.** A foul committed when a player attempts to block from behind by throwing himself across the back or legs of an opposing player other than the runner. Penalty: 15 yards.

**ILLEGAL PROCEDURE.** This indicates several different infractions, the more common being: false start; having less than 7 players on the offensive team's scrimmage line; illegally handing the ball forward; taking more than 2 steps after a fair catch; illegal snap; infraction of substitution rules (College); invalid fair-catch signal (Professional).

**DELAY OF GAME.** Excess time-outs requested or used; illegal delay of game; crawling (High School and College); team not ready to play (College penalty: 15 yards); illegal substitution (High School); interference with opponent or snap of the ball (High School). Penalty: 5 yards.

**ROUGHING-THE-KICKER.** The kicker, or the holder of the ball for the place-kick, has been run into or otherwise illegally interfered with. Penalty: 15 yards.

**ILLEGAL MOTION.** Player or players illegally in motion when the ball is snapped. Penalty: 5 yards.

**PERSONAL FOUL.** Piling on; hurdling; tripping; tackling out-of-bounds; running into opponent obviously out of play; striking; kicking or kneeing an opponent; tackling player who signalled for fair catch; grabbing the face mask of opponent (College). Penalty: 5 yards.

**UNSPORTSMANLIKE CONDUCT.** Besides general unsportsmanlike conduct by player or coach, the signal also indicates: persons illegally on the field; delaying start of either half (High School); invalid signal for a fair catch (College). Penalty: 15 yards.

**ILLEGAL SHIFT.** Player or players failed to stop for one second after a shift. Penalty: 5 yards.

**PERSONAL FOUL.** In Professional football, the referee will give an additional signal to define more precisely the rule infraction.

**ILLEGAL USE OF HANDS.** Penalty: 15 yards.

**INTENTIONAL GROUNDING OF PASS.** Penalty: 15 yards and loss of down.

**INCOMPLETE FORWARD PASS.** The signal also indicates a penalty has been refused; a field-goal or point-after-touchdown kick has been missed.

**TIME-OUT.** In High School and College games, if the official calls for time-out on his own, he taps his chest; in Professional football, the official places one hand on his cap.

**ILLEGALLY PASSING OR HANDING THE BALL FORWARD.** Penalty: 5 yards and loss of down.

**INTERLOCKED INTERFERENCE, OR HELPING THE RUNNER.** Penalty: 15 yards. In Professional football only, crawling: 5-yard penalty.

**PASS OR KICK INTERFERENCE.** Offensive pass interference: 10-yard penalty. Defensive pass interference: Pass ruled completed at spot of foul. Interference with fair-catch opportunity: 15-yard penalty.

**BALL IS DEAD.**

**FIRST DOWN.** The team in possession of the ball has a first down and now has four downs (plays) in which to gain 10 yards for another first down.

**ILLEGAL RECEIVER DOWNFIELD.** Penalty: 10 yards.

**SCORE.** Touchdown, field goal, or place-kick has been made.

**BALL IS READY FOR PLAY.**

**ILLEGALLY KICKING, BATTING, OR TOUCHING BALL.** Illegal kick: 5-yard penalty; illegally kicking ball: 15-yard penalty; illegally kicking or batting free ball: College rules give the offended team possession of the ball at the spot where foul was committed; High School rules call for a 15-yard penalty; forward pass illegally touched: College rules provide for 5 or 15 yards penalty and/or loss of down.

**SAFETY.**

**GAME CLOCK STARTS.**

# OFFICIAL NFL
# DIGEST OF RULES

## FIELD

1. Side lines and end lines are out of bounds. The goal line is actually in the end zone. A player with the ball in his possession scores when the ball is *on, above* or *over* the goal line.
2. The field is rimmed by a white border, six feet wide, along the side lines. All of this is out of bounds.
3. The hash marks (inbound lines) are 70 feet, 9 inches from each side line.
4. Goal posts must be single-standard type, offset from the end line and painted bright gold. The goal posts must be 18 feet, 6 inches wide and the top face of the crossbar must be 10 feet above the ground. Vertical posts extend 30 feet above the crossbar. The actual goal is the plane extending indefinitely *above* the crossbar and between the *outer* edges of the posts.
5. The field is 360 feet long and 160 feet wide. The end zones are 30 feet deep. The line used in try-for-point plays is 2 yards out from the goal line.
6. Chain crew members and ball boys must be uniformly identifiable.
7. All clubs must use standardized sideline markers. Pylons must be used for goal line and end line markings.
8. End zone markers and club identification at 50-yard line must be approved by the Commissioner to avoid any confusion as to delineation of goal lines, side lines and end lines.

## BALL

1. The home club must have 12 balls available for testing by the Referee one hour before game time. In case of bad weather, a playable ball is to be substituted on request of the offensive team captain.

## COIN TOSS

1. The toss of coin will take place within 3 minutes of the kickoff in center of field. The toss will be called by the visiting captain. The winner may choose one of two privileges and the loser gets the other:
   (a) Kick off or receive
   (b) Goal his team will defend.
2. At the end of the first half both captains must appear in center of field to inform the Referee of their choices for the start of the second half. The loser of the toss gets first choice.
3. In case of inclement weather, the toss may be made by the Referee and the two coaches.
4. Both captains must appear in the center of the field three minutes before game time when the Referee will indicate which team is to kick off and which goal the receivers will defend. *No toss is simulated at this time.*

## TIMING

1. The stadium electric clock is official. In case it stops or is being operated incorrectly, the Line Judge takes over the official timing on the field.
2. Each period is 15 minutes. The intermission between the periods is two minutes. Halftime is 15 minutes, unless otherwise specified.
3. On charged team timeouts, the Field Judge starts watch and blows whistle after 1 minute 30 seconds. However, Referee may allow two minutes for injured player and three minutes for equipment repair.
4. Each team allowed three timeouts each half.
5. Offensive team has 30 seconds to put the ball in play. The time is displayed on two 30-second clocks which are visible to players, officials and fans. Field Judge is to call a delay of game penalty (5 yards) when the time limit is exceeded.
6. Clock will start running when ball is snapped following all changes of team possession.

## SUDDEN DEATH

1. The sudden death system of determining the winner shall prevail when score is tied at the end of the regulation playing time of *all NFL games.* The team scoring first during overtime play shall be the winner and the game automatically ends upon any score (by safety, field goal or touchdown) or when a score is awarded by Referee for a palpably unfair act.
2. At the end of regulation time the Referee will immediatley toss coin at center of field in accordance with rules pertaining to the usual pregame toss. The captain of the visiting team will call the toss.
3. Following a 3-minute intermission after the end of the regulation game, play will be continued in 15-minute periods or until there is a score. There is a 2-minute intermission between subsequent periods. The teams change goals at the start of each period. Each team has 3 time outs and general provisions for play in the last 2 minutes of a half shall prevail. Disqualified players are not allowed to return.
   *Exception:* In preseason and regular season games there shall be a maximum of 15 minutes of sudden death with 2 time outs instead of 3. General provisions for play in the last two minutes of a half will be in force.

## TIMING IN FINAL TWO MINUTES OF EACH HALF

1. On kickoff, clock does not start until the ball has been legally touched by player of either team *in the field of play.* (In all other cases, clock starts with kickoff.)
2. A team cannot "buy" an excess timeout for a penalty. However, a *fourth timeout* is allowed without penalty for an injured player, who must be removed immediately. A *fifth timeout* or more is allowed for an injury and a five-yard penalty is assessed if the clock was running. Additionally, if the clock was running and the score is tied or the team in possession is losing, the ball cannot be put in play for at least 10 seconds. The half or game can end while those 10 seconds are run off the clock.

## TRY-FOR-POINT

1. After a touchdown, the scoring team is allowed a try-for-point during one scrimmage down. The ball may be spotted anywhere between the inbounds lines, two or more yards from the goal line. The successful conversion counts one point, whether by run, kick or pass.
2. The *defensive team never can score* on a try-for-point. As soon as defense gets possession, or kick is blocked, ball is dead.
3. Any distance penalty for fouls committed by the defense which prevent the try from being attempted can be enforced on the succeeding kickoff. Any foul committed on a successful try will result in a distance penalty being assessed on the ensuing kickoff.

## PLAYERS SUBSTITUTIONS

1. Each team is permitted 11 men on the field at the snap.
2. Unlimited substitution is permitted. However, players may enter the field only when the ball is dead. Players who have been substituted for are not permitted to linger on the field. Such lingering will be interpreted as unsportsmanlike conduct.
3. Players leaving the game must be out of bounds *on their own side,* clearing the field between the end lines, before a snap or freekick. If player crosses end line leaving field it is delay of game (5-yard penalty).

## KICKOFF

1. The kickoff shall be from the kicking team's 35-yard line at the start of each half and after a field goal and try-for-point. A kickoff is one type of free kick.

2. Either a 1, 2 or 3 inch tee may be used (no tee permitted for field goal or try-for-point plays). The ball is put in play by a placekick or dropkick.
3. If kickoff clears the opponent's goal posts it is *not* a field goal.
4. A kickoff is illegal unless it travels 10 yards OR is touched by the *receiving* team. Once the ball is touched by the receiving team it is a free ball. Receivers may recover and advance. Kicking team may recover but *not* advance *unless* receiver had possession and lost the ball.
5. When a kickoff goes out of bounds between the goal lines without being touched by the receiving team, it must be kicked again. There is a 5-yard penalty for a short kick or an out-of-bounds kick.
6. When a kickoff goes out of bounds between the goal lines and is *touched last* by receiving team, it is receiver's ball at out-of-bounds spot.

## FREE KICK

1. In addition to a kickoff, the other free kicks are a kick after a safety and a kick after a fair catch. In both cases, a dropkick, placekick or punt may be used. (A punt may *not* be used on a kickoff.)
2. On free kick after a fair catch, captain of receiving team has the option to put ball in play by punt, dropkick or placekick *without* a tee, or by snap. If the placekick or dropkick goes between the uprights a field goal is scored.
3. On a free kick after a safety, the team scored upon puts ball in play by a punt, dropkick, placekick without tee. No *score* can be made on a free kick following a safety, even if a series of penalties place team in position. (A field goal can be scored only on a play from scrimmage or a free kick after a fair catch.)

## FIELD GOAL

1. All field goals attempted and missed from scrimmage line beyond the 20-yard line will result in the defensive team taking possession of the ball at the scrimmage line. On any field goal attempted and missed from scrimmage line inside the 20-yard line, ball will revert to defensive team at the 20-yard line.

## SAFETY

1. The important factor in a safety is impetus. Two points are scored for the opposing team when the ball is dead on or behind a team's own goal line *if the impetus came from a player on that team*.
   Examples of safety:
   (a) Blocked punt goes out of kicking team's end zone. Impetus was provided by punting team. The block only changes direction of ball, not impetus (Safety).
   (b) Ball carrier retreats from field of play *into his own end zone* and is downed. Ball carrier provides impetus (Safety).
   (c) Offensive team commits a foul and spot of enforcement is *behind its own goal line* (Safety).
   (d) Player on receiving team muffs punt and, trying to get ball, forces or illegally kicks it into end zone where he or a teammate recovers. He has given new impetus to the ball (Safety).
   Examples of non-safety:
   (a) Player intercepts a pass inside his own 5-yard line and his momentum carries him into his own end zone (No safety). Ball is put in play at spot of interception.
   (b) Player intercepts a pass *in his own end zone* and is downed. Impetus came from passing team, not from defense (Touchback, no safety).
   (c) Player passes from *behind his own goal line*. Opponent bats down ball in end zone (Incomplete pass, no safety).

## MEASURING

1. The forward point of the ball is used when measuring.

## POSITION OF PLAYERS AT SNAP

1. Offensive team must have *at least seven* players on line.
2. Offensive players, not on line, must be at least one yard back at snap. (Exception, player who takes snap.)
3. No interior lineman may move after taking or simulating a three-point stance.
4. No player of either team may invade neutral zone before snap.
5. No player of offensive team may charge or move, after assuming set position, in such manner as to lead defense to believe snap has started.
6. If a player changes his eligibility, the Referee must alert the defensive captain after player has reported to him.
7. All players of offensive team must be stationary at snap, except one back who may be in motion parallel to scrimmage line or backward (not forward).
8. After a shift or huddle all players on offensive team must come to an absolute stop for *at least one second* with no movement of hands, feet, head or swaying of body.
9. A double shift is legal after it has been shown three times in the game outside an opponent's 20-yard line.
10. Lineman may lock legs *only* with the snapper.
11. Quarterbacks can be called for a false start penalty (5 yards) if their actions are judged to be an obvious attempt to draw an opponent offside.

## USE OF HANDS, ARMS AND BODY

1. No player on offense may assist a runner except by blocking for him. There shall be no interlocking interference.
2. A runner may ward off opponents with his hands and arms but no other player on offense may use hands or arms to obstruct an opponent by grasping with hands, pushing or encircling any part of his body during a block.
3. Pass blocking is the obstructing of an opponent by use of the blocker's body above the knee. The hands must be cupped or closed and remain inside the blocker's elbow and inside the frame of the bodies of both the blocker and his opponent. The arms may be in a flexed position but not fully extended to create a push. The blocker may ward off an opponent's attempt to grasp his jersey or arms and prevent contact to his head by up and down action of his flexed arm(s).
4. A *defensive* player may not tackle or hold an opponent other than the runner. He may use his hands and arms only:
   (a) To ward off an obstructing opponent.
       Exception: An eligible receiver is considered to be an obstructing opponent ONLY between line of scrimmage and a point 3 yards beyond unless player who receives snap clearly demonstrates no further intention to pass ball. Beyond this 3-yard limitation a defender may use his hands or arms ONCE in contacting (chucking) a receiver who is in front of him.
   (b) To push or pull opponent out of the way on line of scrimmage.
   (c) In actual attempt to get at or tackle runner.
   (d) To push or pull opponent out of the way in a legal attempt to recover a loose ball.
   (e) During a legal block.
   (f) When legally blocking an eligible pass receiver above the waist.
       When legally blocking an eligible pass receiver above the waist.
       Exception: Eligible receivers lined up within two yards of the tackle, whether on or immediately behind the line, may be blocked below the waist AT or behind the line of scrimmage. NO eligible receiver may be blocked below the waist after he goes beyond the line.

5. A defensive player must not contact an opponent above the shoulders with the palm of his hand *except* during the initial charge or to ward him off on the line. This exception is permitted only if it is not a repeated act against the same opponent during any one contact. In all other cases the palms may be used on head, neck or face *only* to ward off or push an opponent in legal attempt to get at the ball.
6. Any offensive player who pretends to possess the ball or to whom a teammate pretends to give the ball may be tackled provided he is *crossing* his scrimmage line between the ends of a normal tight offensive line.
7. An offensive player who lines up more than 2 yards outside his own tackle may not contact an opponent below the waist if the blocker is moving toward the ball and if contact is made within an area 3 yards on either side of the line.
8. A player of either team may block at any time provided it is not pass interference, fair catch interference or unnecessary roughness.
9. A player may not bat or punch:
   (a) A loose ball (in field of play) *toward* his opponent's goal line or in any direction in either end zone.
   (b) A ball in player possession or attempt to get possession.
   Exception: A forward or backward pass may be batted in any direction at any time by (1) the defense or (2) the offense only to prevent an opponent from intercepting.
10. No player may deliberately kick any ball except as a punt, dropkick or placekick.

## FORWARD PASS

1. A forward pass may be touched or caught only by an eligible receiver. All members of the defensive team are eligible. Eligible receivers on the offensive team are players on either end of line (other than center, guard or tackle) or players at least one yard behind the line at the snap. A T-Formation quarterback is *not* eligible to receive a forward pass during a play from scrimmage.
2. An offensive team may make only *one* forward pass during each play from scrimmage (Loss of down).
3. The passer must be behind his line of scrimmage (Loss of down and 5 yards, enforced from the spot of pass).
4. Only one eligible offensive player may catch a forward pass. If pass is touched by one offensive player and touched or caught by a second eligible offensive player, it is a violation (Loss of down). However, if a forward pass is touched by a *defensive* player before, at same time or after touching by an eligible offensive receiver, *all offensive players then become eligible.*
5. The rules concerning a forward pass and ineligible receivers:
   (a) If ball is touched *accidentally* by an ineligible receiver *on or behind his line* (Loss of down).
   (b) If touched or caught *intentionally* by an ineligible receiver *on or behind his line* (Loss of down and 15 yards).
   (c) If touched or caught (intentionally or accidentally) by ineligible receiver *beyond* the line (Loss of down and 15 yards).
   (d) If ineligible receiver is illegally downfield (10 yards).
6. If a forward pass is caught simultaneously by eligible players on *opposing teams,* possession goes to passing team.
7. Any forward pass becomes incomplete and ball is dead if:
   (a) Pass hits the ground or goes out of bounds.
   (b) Hits the goal post or the cross bar of either team.
   (c) Is caught by offensive player after touching ineligible receiver.
   (d) Is caught by second eligible receiver before being touched by defensive player.
   (e) An illegal pass is caught by the passer.
8. A forward pass is complete when a receiver touches the ground with *both feet* inbounds while in possession of the ball. If a receiver is carried out of bounds by an opponent while in possession in the air, pass is complete at the out-of-bounds spot.
9. If an eligible receiver goes out of bounds accidentally or is forced out by a defender and returns to catch a pass, the play is regarded as a pass caught out of bounds (Loss of down, no yardage).
10. On a *fourth down* pass—when the offensive team is *inside* the *opposition's 20-yard line*—an incomplete pass results in a loss of down at the line of scrimmage.
11. If a personal foul is committed by the *defense* prior to the completion of a pass, the penalty is 15 yards from the spot where ball becomes dead.
12. If a personal foul is committed by the *offense* prior to the completion of a pass, the penalty is 15 yards from the previous line of scrimmage.

## INTENTIONAL GROUNDING OF FORWARD PASS

1. Intentional incompletion of a forward pass is a violation (Loss of down and 15 yards from previous spot). Exception: If the spot of intentional incompletion is on or behind defensive team's goal line during fourth down, and previous spot was inside the opponent's 5-yard line, it is a touchback.
2. It is considered intentional incompletion of a forward pass when the ball strikes the ground after the passer throws, tosses or lobs the ball to prevent a loss of yards by his team.

## PROTECTION OF PASSER

1. No defensive player may run into a passer of a legal forward pass after the ball has left his hand (15 yards). The Referee must determine whether opponent had a *reasonable chance to stop his momentum* during an attempt to block the pass or tackle the passer while he still had the ball. By interpretation, a pass begins when the passer—with possession of ball—starts to bring his hand forward. If ball strikes ground after this action has begun, play is ruled as an incomplete pass. If passer loses control of ball prior to his bringing his hand forward, play is ruled a fumble.

## PASS INTERFERENCE

1. There shall be no interference with a forward pass thrown from behind the line. The restriction for the *passing team* starts *with the snap.* The restriction on the *defensive team* starts when the ball *leaves the passer's hand.* Both restrictions end when the ball is *touched by anyone.*
2. The penalty for *defensive* pass interference is an automatic first down at the spot of the foul. If interference is in the end zone, it is first down for the offense on the defense's 1-yard line. If previous spot was inside the defense's 1-yard line, penalty is half the distance to the goal line.
3. The penalty for *offensive* pass interference is 10 yards from the previous spot.
4. It is interference when any player's movement beyond the passing team's line hinders the progress of an eligible opponent in his attempt to reach a pass. Exception: Such incidental movement or contact when two or more eligible players make a *simultaneous and bona fide* attempt to catch or bat the ball is permitted. "Simultaneous and bona fide" means the contact of an eligible receive and a defensive player when each is playing the ball and contact is unavoidable and incidental to the act of trying to catch or bat the ball.
5. It must be remembered that defensive players have as much right to the *path of the ball* as eligible receivers. Any bodily contact, however severe, is not interference if a

player is making a bona fide and simultaneous attempt to catch or bat the ball.

## BACKWARD PASS

1. Any pass not a forward pass is regarded as a backward pass or lateral. A pass parallel to the line is a backward pass. A runner may pass backward at any time. *Any player on either team* may catch the pass or recover the ball after it touches the ground.
2. A backward pass that strikes the ground can be *recovered* and *advanced* by offensive team.
3. A backward pass that strikes the ground can be recovered but *cannot be advanced* by the *defensive* team.
4. A backward pass *caught in the air* can be *advanced* by the *defensive* team.

## FUMBLE

1. The distinction between a fumble and a muff should be kept in mind in considering rules about fumbles. A fumble is the loss of possession of the ball. A muff is the touching of a loose ball by a player in an unsuccessful attempt to obtain possession.
2. A fumble may be advanced by any player on either team regardless of whether recovered before or after ball hits the ground.
3. On fourth down a fumble (unintentional) inside the defense's 10-yard line during a play from scrimmage, and *not touched* by any defensive player, may be advanced *only by the offensive player fumbling.* If recovered by any other offensive player, the ball is dead at the spot of fumble unless it is recovered behind the spot of fumble. In that case, ball is dead at spot of recovery.

## KICKS FROM SCRIMMAGE

1. Any punt or missed field goal that touches a goal post is dead.
2. During a kick from scrimmage, only the end men, as eligible receivers on the line of scrimmage at the time of the snap, are permitted to go beyond the line before the ball is kicked. Exception: An eligible receiver who, at the snap is aligned or in motion behind the line and more than one yard outside the end man on his side of the line, clearly making him the outside receiver, REPLACES that end man as the player eligible to go downfield after the snap. All other members of the kicking team must remain at the line of scrimmage until the ball has been kicked.
3. Any punt that is blocked and does *not* cross the line of scrimmage can be recovered and advanced by either team. However, if offensive team recovers it must make the yardage necessary for its first down to retain possession if punt was on fourth down.
4. The kicking team may never advance its own kick even though legal recovery is made beyond the line of scrimmage. Possession only.
5. A member of the receiving team may not run into or rough a kicker who kicks from behind his line unless contact is:
   (a) Incidental to and *after* he had touched ball in flight.
   (b) Caused by kicker's own motions.
   (c) Occurs during a quick kick or a kick made after a run or after kicker recovers a loose ball. Ball is loose when kicker muffs snap or snap hits ground.
   (The penalty for *running into* the kicker is 5 yards. For roughing the kicker 15 yards and disqualification if flagrant.)
6. If a member of the kicking team attempting to down the ball on or inside opponent's 5-yard line carries the ball into the end zone, it is a touchback.
7. Fouls during a punt are enforced from the previous spot (line of scrimmage). Exception: Illegal touching, illegal fair catch, invalid fair catch signal, unsportsmanlike conduct after fair catch signal, and fouls by the receiving team during loose ball after ball is kicked (fouls against kicker not included).
8. While the ball is in the air or rolling on the ground following a punt or field goal attempt and receiving team commits a foul before gaining possession, receiving team will retain possession and will be penalized for its foul.
9. It will be illegal for a defensive player to jump on, stand on or be picked up by a teammate in an attempt to block a kick. (Penalty 15 yards, unsportsmanlike conduct).
10. A punted ball remains a kicked ball until it is declared dead or in possession of either team.
11. Any member of the punting team may down the ball anywhere in the field of play. However, it is illegal touching (Official's timeout and receiver's ball at spot of illegal touching). This foul does *not* offset any foul by receivers during the down.
12. Defensive team may advance all kicks from scrimmage (including unsuccessful field goal) whether or not ball crosses defensive team's goal line. Rules pertaining to kicks from scrimmage apply until defensive team gains possession.

## FAIR CATCH

1. The member of the receiving team must raise one arm full length above his head while kick is in flight. (Failure to give proper sign, receivers' ball five yards behind spot of signal.)
2. No opponenet may interfere with the fair catcher, the ball or his path to the ball (15 yards from spot of foul and fair catch is awarded).
3. A player who signals for a fair catch is *not* required to catch the ball. However, if a player signals for a fair catch, he may not block or initiate contact with any player on the kicking team until the ball touches a player (Penalty, snap 15 yards behind spot of foul).
4. If ball hits ground or is touched by member of kicking team in flight, fair catch signal if off and all rules for a kicked ball apply.
5. Any *undue advance* by a fair catch receiver is delay of game. No specific distance is specified for "undue advance" as ball is dead at spot of catch. If player comes to a reasonable stop no penalty (For violation, 5 yards).
6. If time expires while ball is in play and a fair catch is awarded, receiving team may choose to extend the period with one free-kick down. However, placekicker may *not* use tee.

## FOUR ON LAST PLAY OF HALF OR GAME

1. On a foul by *defense* on last play of half or game, the *down is replayed* if penalty is accepted.
2. On a foul by the *offense* on last play of half or game, the *down is not replayed* and the play in which the foul is committed is nullified.
   Exception: Fair catch interference, foul following change of possession, illegal touching. *No score by offense counts.*
3. On *double foul* on last play of half or game, *down is replayed.*

## SPOT OF ENFORCEMENT OF FOUL

There are four basic spots at which a penalty for a foul is enforced:
1. Spot of foul: The spot where the foul is committed.
2. Previous spot: The spot where the ball was put in play.
3. Spot of snap, pass, fumble, return kick or free kick: The spot where the act connected with the foul occurred.
4. Succeeding spot: The spot where the ball next would be put in play if no distance penalty were to be enforced.
   Exception: If foul occurs after a touchdown and before the whistle for a try-for-point, succeeding spot is spot of next kickoff.

5. All fouls committed by offensive team behind the line of scrimmage and in the field of play shall be penalized from the previous spot.
6. When the spot of enforcement for fouls involving defensive holding or illegal use of hands by the defense is behind the line of scrimmage, any penalty yardage to be assessed on that play shall be measured from the line.

### DOUBLE FOUL

1. If there is a double foul *during* a down in which there is a change of possession, the team last gaining possession may keep the ball unless its foul was committed prior to the change of possession.
2. If double foul occurs *after* a change of possession, the defensive team retains the ball at the spot possession was gained.
3. If one of the fouls of a double foul involves disqualification, that player must be removed, but no penality yardage is to be assessed.
4. If the kickers foul during a punt before possession changes and the receivers foul after possession changes, penalties will be offset and the down replayed.

### PENALTY ENFORCED ON FOLLOWING KICKOFF

1. When a team scores by touchdown, field goal, extra point or safety and either team commits a personal foul, unsportsmanlike conduct or obvious unfair act during the down, the penalty will be assessed on the following kickoff.

# NFL SUMMARY OF PENALTIES

### AUTOMATIC FIRST DOWN

1. Awarded to offensive team on all defensive fouls with these exceptions:
   (a) Offsides
   (b) Encroachment
   (c) Delay of game
   (d) Illegal substitution
   (e) Excessive time outs

### LOSS OF DOWN (No yardage)

1. Second forward pass *behind* the line.
2. Forward pass strikes ground, goal post or crossbar.
3. Forward pass goes out of bounds.
4. Forward pass is first touched by eligible receiver who has gone out of bounds and returned.
5. Forward pass touched or caught by second eligible receiver before touched by defense.
6. Forward pass accidentally touches ineligible receiver on or behind line.

### FIVE YARDS

1. Crawling.
2. Defensive holding (automatic first down).
3. Delay of game (if at start of half, 15 yards).
4. Encroachment.
5. Too many time outs.
6. False start.
7. Illegal formation.
8. Illegal shift.
9. Illegal motion.
10. Illegal substitution.
11. Kickoff out of bounds between goal lines and not touched.
12. Invalid fair catch signal.
13. More than 11 players on the field for either team.

14. Less than seven men on offensive line at snap.
15. Offsides.
16. Failure to pause one second after shift or huddle.
17. Running into kicker (automatic first down).
18. More than one man in motion at snap.
19. Grasping face mask of opponent (automatic first down) (15 yards and disqualification if flagrant.)
20. Player out of bounds at snap.
21. Ineligible member(s) of kicking team going beyond line of scrimmage before ball is kicked.

### TEN YARDS

1. Offensive pass interference.
2. Ineligible player downfield during passing down.

### FIFTEEN YARDS

1. Clipping.
2. Fair catch interference.
3. Illegal batting or punching loose ball.
4. Deliberately kicking a loose ball.
5. Illegal crackback block by offense.
6. Piling on (automatic first down).
7. Roughing the kicker (automatic first down).
8. Roughing the passer (automatic first down).
9. Twisting, turning or pulling an opponent by the face mask.
10. Unnecessary roughness.
11. Unsportsmanlike conduct.
12. Delay of game at start of either half.
13. Helping the runner.
14. Holding, illegal use of hands or tripping on offense. Exception: 10-yard penalty if enforced from a spot at or behind line of scrimmage or no deeper than 3 yards downfield.

### FIVE YARDS AND LOSS OF DOWN

1. Forward pass thrown from *beyond* line of scrimmage.

### TEN YARDS AND LOSS OF DOWN

1. Forward pass intentionally touched by ineligible receiver on or behind line.
2. Forward pass intentionally or accidentally touched by ineligible receiver beyond the line of scrimmage.

### FIFTEEN YARDS AND LOSS OF COIN TOSS OPTION

1. Team's late arrival on the field prior to scheduled kickoff.

### FIFTEEN YARDS AND LOSS OF DOWN

1. Intentional grounding of forward pass (cannot score a safety).

### FIFTEEN YARDS (AND DISQUALIFICATION IF FLAGRANT)

1. Striking opponent with fist.
2. Kicking or kneeing opponent.
3. Striking opponent on head or neck with forearm, elbow or hands.
4. Entering game a second time with illegal equipment.
5. Roughing kicker.
6. Roughing passer.
7. Malicioius unnecessary roughness
8. Unsportsmanlike conduct.
9. Palpably unfair act (Distance penalty determined by the Referee after consultation with other officials).

### SUSPENSION FROM GAME AND FIVE YARDS

1. Illegal equipment. (Player may return after one down when legally equipped.)